100 ENCOURAGEMENTS & EXHORTATIONS

MIKE STERNAD

100 ENCOURAGEMENTS & EXHORTATIONS #1

By Mike Sternad

Published by Contented Life Publishing

Calvary Chapel Mobile
Website: www.calvarychapelmobile.com

Mailing Address: 312 T Schillinger Rd. S, Mobile, AL 36608
Phone: 251-287-1253
E-mail: mikesternad@gmail.com

ISBN: 9781734345445

Unless otherwise indicated, Scripture quotations in this book are taken from the New King James Version of the Bible. Copyright © 1979, 1980, 1982 by Thomas Nelson, Inc., Publishers. Used by permission.

Edited by Elizabeth-Mae Morse
Interior Design by Ulrika Towgood

Printed in the United States of America

INTRODUCTION

I have learned so much from the Lord over the years. He has spoken to my heart encouragements and exhortations that have opened my eyes to shape me into the believer I am today. As I've served the Lord, He has lifted me up when I have been down and called me to action when I thought I was counted out. I love the words He has spoken to me and want to relay them to you with the hope and prayer that you too are lifted up, encouraged and exhorted.

As you read each exhortation and encouragement, the Lord may bring to mind a scripture, a memory, an admonition, or a prayer. Write them down in the lines provided so you can remember the things God has shown you and reflect on His Word to you.

But exhort one another daily, while it is called "Today," lest any of you be hardened through the deceitfulness of sin. Hebrews 3:13

1 **Contentment in the present is possible all because of what God has already done for you.** People search their whole lives for happiness and never find it, because they don't look to the Lord eternal. Contentment cannot be found by looking to people, places or things on this earth. It can only be found by looking to God above. As you reflect on your past, you will see that God has already radically worked in your life. His hand was upon you and He was there when you needed Him the most. God has led you every step of the way.

_____

_____

_____

2 **When you feel like a wreck, know that God is still working.** There are many moments when you may feel horrible and don't want to face another day. You may feel tired thinking your life is chaotic and discombobulated. During these moments, you must remember that the Lord does not take a day off. He is constantly working on your heart and in your life circumstances. You must believe it!

_____

_____

_____

3 **Don't let hobbies hijack the time you could spend with the Lord.** Hobbies can be good and healthy as long as they don't completely consume you. A good thing can become a very bad thing if it becomes all-consuming. Enjoy your hobbies, but don't let them take you away from the Lord and hijack that precious one-on-one time with God. He longs for daily communication with you and when you spend time with Him, you are blessed abundantly!

_____

_____

_____

4 **Decimate discouraging thoughts. Keep your mind on your Maker.** The mind can wander in a split second, and so you must make concentrated effort to keep your mind on Christ. The enemy will fill your thoughts with doubt and cause you to question everything you know to be true. But God has already transformed your mind. Now it is up to you to focus on Him and the eternal. Remember, discouraging thoughts are never from the Lord, but encouraging thoughts are always from Him. So don't buy into the devil's lies. Believe the truth from God always.

_____

_____

_____

5 **When God calls you to step up, don't give up.**
The tendency in our culture is to give up when things get difficult. There is no doubt that life is hard, but remember God can handle it. He's not worried so neither should you be. Failure is a part of life. What is important is that you learn from it, grow and keep moving forward. The only thing that will grow from success is your ego, but failure will lead to a strengthened faith and determination to forge ahead in the name of Jesus.

_____

_____

_____

6 **To eradicate spiritual apathy, dig daily into God's Word.** Reading the Bible has pulled me out of the depths of despair more than just a few times! As you get into God's Word, apathy dissipates and passion emerges. Your countenance lifts and your passion becomes more fervent. I absolutely love the Word of God and the more I get into it, the more it fires me up and prepares me for God's calling on my life. So get into God's Word and let it seep into your heart and transform you.

_____

_____

_____

7 **When it comes to evangelism, you don't control the outcome. You are simply called to get out there and share God's unending love unconditionally.** You plant and you water, like the Bible says, but God gives the increase. You are not working on commission, but on salary. In other words, God is not expecting you to change anyone's heart; He is expecting you to relay the reality of the gospel. He does the rest. He closes the deal. He transforms. You just inform.

_____

_____

_____

8 **Even in difficult times, there is so much for us to be thankful for.** I would seriously recommend making a list of everything you are grateful for. God has blessed His children in so many ways that it is hard to keep track of all of them! We innately take things for granted which is why we must remind ourselves of all that God has done in our lives. There will be difficult times, but we have already been delivered. We are not victims at all—we are victors in Christ. It is time to live like it!

_____

_____

_____

9 **Active faith will crowd out fear and destroy doubt**. Sitting on the sidelines while watching others in the game of God's will is the avenue to letting doubt and unbelief overtake you. If you are not active for the Lord, your faith will flounder. If you are active for the Lord, your faith will flourish. The question is, *are you in or out of the game?* Are you going to be bold and live for God or be anxious and live for self? I encourage you to go all in for the Lord today. It is amazing!

_____

_____

_____

10 **Don't seek worldly affirmation from people. Seek the Lord for heavenly confirmation.** Don't live to get a pat on the back from man; live to please the Lord! People are faulty and they will fail you. You are faulty and you will fail people. We are all imperfect human beings. So abandon expectations from people and forget worldly affirmation. Instead, seek God daily for confirmation in what He has called you to do with each season. I believe this is the way God wants every believer to live.

_____

_____

_____

11 **Your priorities will be in line when you are aligned with the Lord.** As you get on the road of God's will through obedience to Him, your priorities will be on point. When you do your own thing and close your ears and eyes off to what God is doing, you'll go astray. I don't know about you, but I want to be in the dead center of God's mission for me. The avenue to get to that place is through the constant obedience to and toward the Lord.

_____

_____

_____

12 **Get off the self-led path and onto the God-led path. It's worth every step.** When you attempt to control your own destiny, it can lead to major destruction. Sounds dramatic, right? But the fact is that the Lord wants to lead you as a believer and when you are in the middle of His mission for you, you'll realize that God's ways are so much better than your ways. It's a simple truth but an awesome reality.

_____

_____

_____

13 **The power of the Lord never rests on the vessel. It flows through you, and glorifies Him.**
Everything you do can actually glorify God. You and I never have the right to claim any power over anything. God is the source and fountainhead of power. Being a vessel and allowing the Lord to fill you, and then for you to pour out His attributes to a world that needs hope—that's humility. You are not on planet earth to take credit for anything good that you do. When you see great things happen, it is God doing the work and so give Him the credit, honor, and glory. Let His power flow through you today!

_____

_____

_____

14 **In following God, have patience in the waiting and passion in the working.** You may have lost your patience a few times this past week and your passion for the things of God may have lessened. So how do we remain patient and live with godly passion?

I believe we do this by consistently being in God's Word and staying plugged into a local church. Don't church hop thinking you'd find a perfect church. It's not going to happen. Let God lead you to a church where you'll get fed the Word of God. Pray and fellowship with believers who will actually point you to Jesus often. Stay connected and committed.

15 **May you not take God's Word for granted.** Stand strong in the Scriptures. Make sure the church you're going to is based and founded upon the Word of God, rather than on man's opinion. Read the Bible more than you read any other book. Stay open to how God wants to speak to you, correct you and encourage you from His Word. Sometimes we just go through the motions and read God's Word as if it were a novel. The Bible is much more than that—it is God-breathed. The Word of God is living, and your God speaks to you through every page. Stand strong in the Scriptures and stay consistent in the Lord's Word!

16 **It's so freeing when you make God's Word the groundwork for your life.** Many times we think we have to figure life out on our own with no help from anyone. The truth is that you have the Word of God as the blueprint for building your life on Christ. I'm not to be burdened with attempting to be strategic and clever in order to navigate through life. I have the manual! Following God's Word allows me to be free from the burden of trying to build my spiritual life alone.

_____

_____

_____

17 **You're passing through this temporary world heralding a permanent hope.** Your life on earth will not last forever. Sometimes we live like this earth is our permanent and everlasting home. The truth is life is fleeting and we are not here forever. You and I were not created to settle down on earth and build our little kingdoms here. We were made for more. This earth is our temporary waiting room until we go in to see the Doctor, get completely healed and live forever. Heaven is our home. Yet, while we're here on this earth, we are blessed to reflect Christ and let people know that life is about Jesus. Share the gospel as you are passing through this world.

_____

_____

_____

18 **Keep the faith and forge ahead knowing God is with you.** At times, it may feel like you cannot take one more step forward. It may feel like you are hitting a wall, that God is silent, that circumstances never seem to be good or pleasant. Trust God. You may be in a season of storms right now. But to forge ahead through the thickest storms, you need to keep on the forefront of your heart and mind that God is with you. It's about trusting Him through every day and every season of your life. As you look to Jesus, your faith will stay solid and you will press forward no matter what. True spiritual growth takes time especially as you are being tested through trials! Keep looking up and keep looking ahead.

_____

_____

_____

19 **God is your active refuge in this misaligned world.** You may have run until you've fallen over and lost your breath in exhaustion. Instead of finding your shelter and refuge in the Lord, you have kept going falsely believing that you are unstoppable. This world may commend you for working eighty hours a week with no sleep. It may seem like you are better than others because you just won't quit. But the reality is a person who keeps running that pace will soon get discouraged and burned out. Don't let this world dictate how you live. Let the Lord lead you. Make sure to work but also rest.

_____

_____

_____

20 **Difficulties do not deplete you of the Lord's blessings.** Sometimes it may seem like your problems are overshadowing God's mercies and the result is depression and defeat. The way to get out of this self-inflicted rut is to not let your difficulties overtake your life or guide your decisions. To focus only on your perceived problems will leave you doubting and drained of any and all energy. Exhaustion is the result of running your race without the Lord. It just doesn't work. Keep your eyes on Jesus and know that you will get through whatever challenges you are facing presently.

_____

_____

_____

21 **You are a work in progress.** Praise God for His grace. If you are reading this, you are alive and if you are alive, God wants to continue to refine you. The Lord is not done with you no matter where you came from and how old or young you are. There is no point where God ceases to work on your heart. You are a work in progress and that means there are always more areas and more ways for you to grow in the faith!

_____

_____

_____

22 **Don't let worry wreck you.** Trust God and let your worry be eradicated. I've never seen anything built and thrive due to worry and anxiety. Worry, if left unchecked, will completely ruin your countenance and lead to major stress and depression. Some people think it's their job to worry. It's not. The way to eradicate and sideline worry is to trust in God on a day-to-day basis. Sometimes it's minute-by-minute since life can be chaotic and overwhelming. You can't just stop worrying magically. You must trust God in order for worry to wane and dwindle away. Depending on the Lord for everything will lead to a confidence and boldness that this world cannot give you. Trust Him.

_____

_____

_____

23 **May generosity be a habit that you emulate from the Lord.** God is a giver. In our selfish American culture, there is a tendency to believe that the more a person has, the better off he is. Not true! The amount of stuff you have doesn't equate to what kind of person you are! God calls you to not hoard, but to help out by giving yourself to those who are in need. You have the privilege of giving out what God has graciously given to you. Is that amazing or what? God is a giver and He is our example. As Jesus walked this earth, He gave out truth non-stop, He gave of His time,

He gave love and compassion—and we see the powerful effects of His actions. May you be a giver and in doing so, see lives altered and transformed.

_____

_____

_____

24 **To relieve uneasiness and alleviate anxiety, depend upon the Lord.** When you try and take on the burdens and pressures of life, you'll be left stressed out and burnt out. You were not created to carry every difficulty that comes your way. To trust in the Lord means to let Him carry your burdens and cares. Independence is a worldly concept that promotes needing no one. As believers, you are not to be ashamed to be desperate for God because yes, He is your crutch, your wheelchair and your gurney! You depend upon Him because He is a God of love and He is your only hope and help. What a blessing!

_____

_____

_____

25 **Don't let storms bring stress.** Your Creator can keep you calm through any conflict. If the weather of life seems to be darkening around you, look up! The only way to sincerely smile through a storm is to look to the Lord and obtain your joy from Him. When chaos arises, make sure your grip is on the eternal and not on the earthly. Storms are not meant to bring stress. They are meant to clear your path and make a way to the road of God's will that you did not see before. When your comfort comes from the Creator of the universe, conflict will mean little to you. He is more than able.

---

26 **Surrendering to God will crowd out your fear and refill you with faith.** To give up your whole life to the Lord is the beginning of freedom and victory. Freedom from fear and victory over timidity. Surrendering will activate your faith to such a degree that you'll follow the Lord wholeheartedly. It's not easy to surrender your life on a daily basis, but it is necessary if you want God to use you in great and mighty ways. All glory to Him!

---

27 **Order of priorities in life. God first. Others next. You last.** With the world it is actually the exact opposite. You first, others next, God last. What a sad state this world is in, but remember this world does not dictate who you are or what actions you take. Let God lead you and know that He honors your daily decision to put Him first, others next and yourself last. In no way does this negate you taking care of yourself; it demonstrates Jesus' example of being the One true others-centered Person who ever lived on this earth. May we follow suit!

_____

_____

_____

28 **It takes daily surrender to be in step with God's will.** Let Him take control. You may be a person who wants to be in control all the time. If that's you, then it is not easy to give up control to God and trust Him for everyday life. Yet, it is the best action you can take especially knowing that God is sovereign and knows exactly what He is doing! I want to be in step with the Lord in this life. In order for me to be that, I have to intentionally make an effort to get up and give the day to the Lord, entrusting Him with the conversations I will have and the things I'm called to do. The more I trust God, the more my stress will dissipate.

_____

_____

_____

29 **May you abandon self-trust and embrace God's plan.** Trust Him. He has you. Sometimes you live as if you don't need the Lord. I promise you I'm not trying to make you feel bad, but the fact is that we sometimes think we can do it ourselves. Independence becomes a regular occurrence and then there ceases to be room for the Lord. Faith can't be activated if you are constantly walking by sight. When you fully accept that God is truly leading your life and you _let_ Him take control, the pressure is off. Stress is dissipated and anxiety vanishes. Don't trust in yourself—trust in the Lord!

_____

_____

_____

30 **Living out God's calling for your life leads to abundant joy and true contentment.** You'll know what God wants you to do if you are seeking Him through prayer and through His Word. The result of focusing on the Lord and following Him is a heart that is truly happy. It sounds so simple, but I think we often make it too complicated. If you are being obedient to the Lord, then you are in His will. If you are consistently seeking Him, then you'll know what He's calling you to do from season to season. Abandon self and embrace God.

_____

_____

_____

31 **To be in line with the Lord, you have to be in line with Scripture.** God will never lead you to do something that is contradictory to Scripture. Ever. There are some things that you don't have to pray about, especially if the Bible disagrees with them. There are gray areas where you must seek the Lord on what direction to go, what to do or what not to do. But the Lord will never call you to compromise the truth in order to do His Work. This is the action that believers engage in when they don't want to follow the truth and instead want to do what they want to do. Know your Bible and follow it. The Word says not to gossip, lie or cheat, so don't. We as Christians must stop disobeying the Bible and justifying what we are or are not doing. Always stick to the Scriptures!

_____

_____

_____

32 God will hear and respond to your prayers no matter how small you think they are. Our human understanding is so small and limited. There are some things that we don't even pray about, because we think they are not as important as other bigger and more lofty issues. The Bible makes it clear that we are to pray often and about everything. Persevere in prayer and know that God wants you to come to Him with even the smallest matters! Don't be timid. Pray and storm the gates of heaven and seek God like never before!

_____

_____

_____

33 If you don't mourn over your sin, you may be complacent toward it. It's such a good thing to mourn over your own sin, because then you are sincerely sorrowful over your disobedience to God! That is a good thing. If you didn't feel bad for going against the ways of the Lord, then you would feel bad only that you got caught—not that you did wrong. Have a heart that is in tune with God's truth; a heart that repents quickly!

_____

_____

_____

34 **A small portion of the Lord's strength can get you through the biggest trials.** God created the universe and He created you. He loves His creation and deeply cares about what you go through. God is *not* indifferent. Ever. As you face serious conflicts in life, know that the Lord is all you need to lean upon for dear life. He will hold you up and if need be, carry you. God is strong and His ways are so much better than your ways. Trials will continue to come into your life, but as the Lord is in your heart, trust Him to get you through. Lean upon Him to give you strength

_____

_____

_____

35 **When evangelizing, you are simply called to share the truth; you aren't called to control the results.** This should take the pressure off of you! The Lord has called you to share the gospel, not to save anyone. You are a vessel through whom the truth runs in order to reach people who need to be saved.

You should never feel burdened to yield results because you cannot do anything about them. You are a messenger who relays a message that can transform a life by saving a soul. You have heard the truth. Now you get to share it and follow up with prayer.

_____

_____

_____

36 **Every daily decision you make can lead to either deliverance or destruction.** Choose wisely. Sounds like a lot of pressure, doesn't it?! It is true. Decisions matter so much to our immediate future that it is super critical to make decisions with God not only integrated in those decisions, but leading the way! I'm sure there have been times in your life when you made a decision or began walking down a path, and you realized you did not even consult with the Lord. The result was confusion, disorientation and defeat. It is never wise to make any decisions without the Lord. He is the One who knows what decisions we should make and which direction we should go. Please don't forget that!

_____

_____

_____

37 **God's not only there in the bad times—He's with you in the victorious times as well.** When you are able to overcome difficulties in your life, God doesn't flee just because you are doing well. He stays right there with you rejoicing because He has given you the strength and wisdom to triumph and have a breakthrough! Isn't it amazing how God celebrates your victories with you? He is not only with you, but He is for you! Please believe that the Lord, the Creator of the universe, is with you through the major storms and through the crisp, clear days!

---

38 **Don't let drama cause division and derail you. Let the drama die.** Drama is such a waste of time. Life is too short to get caught up in the minutiae happening around you. Ignore the pettiness and focus on the more serious, eternal facets of life. Don't allow strife to sidetrack you from what God is calling you to do. It is destructive and has no place in the church or in your life. Let it go and go forward with the Lord!

---

39 **God wants to give you peace in the midst of your problems.** I know it's hard for you at times, because life is so busy and there are so many things you have to juggle! Even vacation can seem frenzied and you come home more tired than when you left. You need to slow down but you just have a lot going on. Remember this. The Lord Jesus wants to give your heart peace in the most intense and seemingly overwhelming moments. He can and wants to give you peace. The key is to let Him.

_____

_____

_____

40 **Love one another despite differences.** It's such a great fact that you are different and unique from everyone else on this planet. God didn't make a mistake when He made you. He knew exactly what He was doing as He did with every other human being on the face of this earth. Therefore, God's heart is that we treat everyone as created and loved by God, because they are! There is no reason to treat someone differently just because they are not similar to you. The thread that always stays the same is the truth that God loves all. So love others and don't be afraid to connect with those who are totally different than you for the Lord may want to reach that person through you!

_____

_____

_____

41 **Division is loathsome because it stems from the flesh**. Some people will disagree with you and care less about making peace. These people may be professional bridge burners and want nothing to do with you. Instead of being forgiving and conciliatory, they prefer to hold grudges, be angry and let that root of bitterness grow out of control. This mentality is not of God and is totally unbiblical. And the amount of stress and anxiety that results from this mindset is so unhealthy.

While you may not be able to fix everything on your end, if you do what you can to make peace God will give you rest in your heart and mind. The flesh feeds off of feelings and emotions that creep in and seek to destroy any semblance of heart rest. Starve the flesh and feed your soul—the result will be such a blessing.

_____

_____

_____

42 **Empathy is possible when you are eternally minded.** You've dealt with difficult people throughout your life and sometimes you just want to walk away. The fact is that without the Lord, things people say and do will get to you and stress you out. The way to change that mindset is to see people as God sees them. He created each person and so loves each one and desires that they be saved. Empathy will fill your heart when you catch the heart of God for humanity. Don't give up on people but have grace upon them just as God has grace upon you! Even those who are nasty and ugly toward you are children of God, so make sure to go out of your way to reach out to them. They may resist and reject you but keep focusing on the eternal by praying for them.

---

43 **It is biblical for you to be expectant of God to do great things.** When you expect a lot out of people, you are setting yourself up for complete letdowns and disappointments. But it is very spiritually healthy to expect God to do the miraculous, to move in difficult situations, and to work greatly in your life. After all, you can do small things without the Lord, but great things come from God. When you truly believe that God can do the miraculous, you'll not see impossibilities anymore. Instead, you'll see that God can and will work no matter what.

---

44 **Being exhausted for eternity is so fulfilling.** Your goal is never to get as tired as you can while serving the Lord, but the reality is that you will get tired in doing God's work and will! Yes, you have rest in your heart from Jesus, but you are to keep your hand to the plow and serve the Lord full-heartedly— never half-heartedly. Give your all for the sake of the kingdom and continue to reach out to lost souls and hurting people. You can be both tired and fulfilled from doing the Lord's work. Make sure you do get physical rest, but always giving your all unto the Lord.

_____

_____

_____

45 **Love is a great indicator that you are living for eternity.** If you lack love and are just angry and bitter all the time, then biblically you are not living the way God intended you to live. You should be in the midst of joy on a regular basis! If not, you may be focused on other things rather than on the Lord. Are you reflecting the love of Jesus or are you portraying Him as a tyrant? How is your heart and attitude on a daily basis? It is a great action to assess your own heart to see where you're at with the Lord and identify weaknesses. Then you can ask the Lord to be your strength in those areas. Reflect love.

_____

_____

_____

46 **Every day is an opportunity for you to go all out for the Lord.** To go all out for the Lord is to prioritize living for Him first and letting Him lead your day-to-day schedule. It is to live with the motivation to please Him rather than to please people. You see, in serving God you may ruffle some feathers and it may cause people to mock or criticize you. That's OK. Let those opinions of you go. You and I are not living to attempt to make everyone we meet happy. We are living to fulfill our calling while on this earth, and time is super short. Don't hold back. God's gifted you in certain ways and you are called to use those gifts to glorify the Lord and in turn, affect lives for Him. There are God-given opportunities in front of you every day. Take them.

_____

_____

_____

47 **Don't let conflict complicate your relationship with the Lord.** Sometimes when you allow discouraging thoughts that stem from conflict to ruminate in your mind, your relationships get complicated. You begin to stress out and freak out. Things don't seem in line; your life feels chaotic and messy. What should be simple has turned complicated and brings anxiety, stress and an array of negative emotions. The way to deal with conflict is to seek the Lord for resolution and then leave it in His hands. Don't carry burdens that you are not called to carry. Grow in the action of letting go of the past and the result will be freedom to move forward. Keep it simple.

_____

_____

_____

48 **The Christian life is not about strict rules—it's about a solid relationship with God.** If you feel like your walk of faith is all about a rote set of rules that you must follow or God will be mad at you, that's the wrong mindset. The Law was given to demonstrate to you that you are not good without God. I'm not trying to be mean, but the fact is the Ten Commandments were written as a standard to live by. The more you live out your faith, and the more mature you become in Christ, the more you realize that you cannot keep these commandments. We are sinners in need of the Savior.

These rules will teach you that you need to stop striving and start surrendering. Your relationship with the Lord will strengthen as you cling to Him and communicate with Him. It's not about rules. It's about relationship.

_____

_____

_____

49 **Your trials may be intense, but so is God's strength.** You've been through some serious and unbelievable difficulties. I'm sure you've faced storms that you thought would tear you down and take you out. There have been moments of stress and maybe anxiety that have threatened your spiritual life as the enemy was working overtime to get you away from God's will. Please remember and remind yourself that God is stronger than any storm you will ever face. He will sustain you and get you through those intense trials. Trust Him and believe that He will even use those tough times to refine your heart and life. He is mighty, powerful and more than capable of getting you through every situation!

_____

_____

_____

50 **Don't look for a pat on the back. Live to please the Lord.** You are not to try to get approval from people. You are to get in line with God's will and His ways. Of course, to your flesh it feels good to get approval from people, but that should never be your main goal. Walk on the path of His purpose. As you live your life for the Lord, He is pleased and you are blessed. Those who are excited to see you walk in His calling will be blessed too. It may make others mad or jealous, because they are not walking in God's will, but regardless of what people think of you, keep running your race on the roadmap God has given you. Please don't let anyone or anything stop you from living to please the Lord.

_____

_____

_____

51 **Not every opportunity is from the Lord.** Pray for discernment to know which opportunities are from within and which opportunities are from above. Just because something is good does not mean it's God's will. The way to discern is to seek the Lord for clear confirmation through the avenues in which He speaks to you. Opportunity can sometimes cloud the Lord's calling in your life so you must be aware that not everything before you is an open door. Sometimes the door is shut and you try and pry it open or the Lord has locked the door and you attempt to pick it. Don't force what God hasn't called you to, but also don't just take every opportunity presented to you without avidly seeking God.

_____

_____

_____

52 **Your life is so short. Make it count.** You are going to die. I promise I'm not trying to be melodramatic, but the fact is ten out of ten people will die! The Bible is clear that our time on this earth is super short; and so we must redeem the time and use what time we have left wisely. When you're older I know you don't want to look back filled with regrets because you half-heartedly lived for the Lord. You want to use your life fully for God and fulfill those goals that He clearly gives you from day to day. Life is short and God doesn't want you to waste those moments. What not to do is beat yourself up over those missed moments you had before you. Instead, use those moments as opportunities to realize that next time you will not be silent. You'll speak up and share the truth that transformed your heart.

_____

_____

_____

53 **Live like you matter to God, because you do.**
At times you may feel undervalued and over-looked. Please don't buy into that mindset because it's not from God. He does not think you are a bother or that you are in the way of His plans. The Lord absolutely loves you, values you and sees you as one of a kind. You can be confident in the Lord because He sees you as a part of His plan and He will equip you to enact and fulfill that plan. You matter to God so much and He loves you immensely! Believe it!

_____

_____

_____

54 **You have one life to live. Live it for the Lord who loves you.** This life is here and gone. It is a flash and before you know it, you'll be at the latter end reflecting back on the moments you've experienced. As the years fly by, the worst thing you can do is look back and regret what you didn't do or what you could have done differently.

Your time is valuable, especially when you are using it to glorify and honor the Lord. God loves you so much and wants to see you being a doer of the Word, letting people know about His heart and how good He is. Time is short. Live your life fully for God!

_____

_____

_____

55 **Don't back down from opposition. Use God's strength to stand firm.** The haters can actually be used in your life to spur you on to live for the Lord even more devotedly. Oftentimes your worst criticizers are those who are doing nothing for the Lord. They think their job is to point out sin in others and judge and slander them. That is not a gift of the Spirit. Opposition will come, but the Lord is already with you, defending you and protecting you. The strength that is authentic and always available is the strength that comes straight from God.

_____

_____

_____

56 **Now is the time to live out your purpose, because yesterday is over.** The past is overrated and focused on entirely too much. The fact is your past is over. The only things you should bring with you from the past are those moments where the Lord worked radically and came through in your situation. You have those turning points in your life where the Lord broke through your situation and did the miraculous. Yesterday is done so live for your purpose presently. God wants to use your life in amazing ways right where you are now. Being overly future focused will lead to disappointment and disillusionment, because our attention is not directed toward God's present leading. Live for the Lord today for yesterday is over and tomorrow isn't here yet.

_____

_____

_____

57 **Wisdom has never come from what is ahead. It comes from Who is above.** Life may bring you some experiences that help you for future moments, but the wisdom you need to navigate presently, as well as in the future, is straight from God. Look up on a regular basis especially when you must make decisions and have no clue what to do. The average person makes thousands of decisions each day and you want to make sure that you are consulting and seeking God for the direction of those decisions! Well-meaning opinions from others will never set you on the road to God's will. Instead, they may just get you confused and lost. If you want to stay in the middle of God's mission for you, seek Him before making moves in this life.

_____

_____

_____

58 **Your reaction can either be a great witness or a missed opportunity.** People will say and do the craziest things sometimes. Your reaction to the craziness actually matters. Just by how you react to a certain joke, comment or ungodly action by another can either reinforce or ruin your witness.

It makes me think of those bracelets from the 1980s with the letters WWJD. *What would Jesus do?* This question can cause you to think about your actions and reactions beforehand as you ask yourself, *Am I being a good witness by the actions I take in response to the events around me and the words spoken to me?* Don't be paranoid about how you are behaving, but don't just disregard your conduct either. How we react actually matters to God! Pray for strength and wisdom in the way you react toward this dim and fallen world. Be the light by what you say and do in response to others.

_____

_____

_____

59 **Whether you like it or not, you influence a lot of people.** You have the blessing of being an imperfect influence who inspires others to follow a perfect God. So as you live your life for the Lord and walk out your faith, know that you are having an impact on more people than you think! If your goal and aim is to please God, others will see it and want to emulate that. This is an eye-opener that everything you do and say actually matters and can pull people closer to the Lord. So be the light that reflects His heart and His actions. Be the influence that causes people to ask why you are smiling through storms and how you are blessed through bad times. Shine!

_____

_____

_____

60 **Your past is simply a tool to testify of how God is incredibly gracious.** Don't despise the testimony of how God has saved you and set you apart for Himself. Use it as an avenue to share the heart of God to people who do not know Him. You don't have to share every detail of your past. Only share what you are comfortable with. I have used my past a ton of times to bring encouragement to people who think there is no hope or feel their loved one will never accept the Lord. But not so! There is always hope. So use your testimony as a tool to relay God's character to the lost.

_____

_____

_____

61 **Yesterday's actions don't define today's triumphs.** Don't live in past victories, because the past is over and God has new victories for you to walk in. Some believers are still talking about that one time years ago when they shared the gospel with that person and they got saved. That is amazing but God has new adventures for you to walk in and even more people to share the gospel with. Much of the time when we talk about letting the past go, we think of those horrible actions we have done. But it also applies to those amazing times when God used us for His glory! Yes, remember those times, but don't live in them or you'll get stuck in the past and be inactive for Jesus in the present. Live in the now and see what God has for you presently.

_____

_____

_____

62 **Know the truth and tell others.** When you are excited about something, you can't help but to tell someone! You're bursting at the seams to relay the information to anyone who would listen. You know that God's Word has transformed your mind, changed your life and set you free. You know that nothing is more exciting than that. So you are so blessed to relay that to others so that God can set them free.

Being a truth teller is a blessing, not a burden. The more you dig into the Scriptures, the more you realize it is all about Jesus and His people telling other people about God! It isn't an obligation for you. It's an opportunity. So get out there and tell the truth to others!

---

63 **Live out what you've taken in.** Talk is useless if it doesn't line up with your actions. You can say something one minute, but then turn around and do something contrary the next minute. As believers we don't ever claim to be even close to perfect, but we do want to live out what comes out of our mouths. Unbelievers already believe we are hypocrites; we do not want to feed that false assumption. You have the great opportunity to live out what God is working into your heart and life. It is an absolute blessing to read God's Word, have it speak to us, and implement it! You are not to be pressured or stressed as you try to follow the Word. But you are to consistently read and apply it to your life on a day-to-day basis. People will see this and your light will shine in this life! Read and heed!

---

64 **The Bible is your basis of truth, your blueprint for life, and your instruction manual before leaving earth.** You have the most amazing resource at your disposal whenever you want it. The Bible is the most sold, most stolen, and most overlooked book in the entire world. As you read it, it gives you all the information you need to lead you through a steady transformation in your life.

When I began reading the Bible, my eyes were opened to the truths I'd been searching for my whole life. You see, it is not a philosophy book full of questions. It is God's words chock full of answers. Let it be your basis of truth and blueprint for life as He works it beautifully into your heart. But remember, your Bible is not a weapon to bring hurt to people, but a tool to bring them healing. So dive into it and let it seep into your very being.

_____

_____

_____

65 **Belief opens up the infinite.** When you sincerely and genuinely believe what God says in His Word, it will open more than just your spiritual eyes. It will also open the whole eternal realm and you'll begin to see things from a brand new vantage point! This is both amazing and sobering. Amazing because the Lord has allowed you to peer into eternal things and clearly understand what life is actually about. And sobering because you see what goes on in the spiritual battle when the spiritual realm is opened up!

Faith is the channel that flows from the natural to the supernatural. It is so amazing, we don't want to close our eyes or we'll miss it. May we seek God and continue to see clearly that there is a whole eternal realm that takes priority over the physical. Believe it and watch what God does.

_____

_____

_____

66 **Faith won't falter as long as you consistently feed it.** Those moments when your faith breaks down are a result of not living out God's Word. You don't want your faith to waver nor do you want it to crumble because of the pressures of this world. Your faith will flourish as you stay active living for Jesus and you'll keep inspired as you both hear and heed Him.

When the core of who you are is filled with the Word, you can let your heart direct your actions. Consistently feed your soul with spiritual nourishment from heaven and resist toxic worldly ideas that the enemy uses to distract you. Don't let your faith falter, but let it be built up and strengthened from season to season. Trials aren't there to break your faith. They are there to build your faith and make you stronger in Him than ever before.

---

67 The future is bright if you embrace the present.

You will live your life fully when you aren't stuck in the past or obsessed about the future. Live for today because the time is now.

You may have procrastinated and put off the work the Lord has for you, but may that stop today. You have heard the saying, "Live for the present," but I say, "Live for God presently." He is not looking for you to have faith at some point in the future. He is looking for you to have faith in the here and now. Give your all to the Lord. Embrace your circumstances because where you are is where He wants you. Press in and don't fight it. See how He works because He *will* work. You will produce fruit where you're planted. Today is the day.

---

68 **Lean into the storm and watch God calm it.**
There are life moments when you know you are going to be in the midst of a storm. There are life events you just cannot control. During these very moments, keep going forward and know that the road of God's will is not going to be problem free.

Your tendency may be to run at every sign of trouble, but sometimes God allows a storm so you can learn to navigate through it. Just know that as you do, God will be with you and will eventually calm your storm. Your heart can stay calm no matter how intensely the storm rages because Jesus lives in your heart. He has you. He is in control.

_____

_____

_____

69 **Don't forget to wait on the Lord.** Sometimes we forget that God's timing is way better than our timing. Your timing is imperfect. Mine is too. The reality is none of us have the right timing apart from the Lord! His timing is the absolute best!

Being rash is never a good thing. When you forget to wait upon Him, you get ahead of Him and you make yourself out to be wiser than Him. The fact is you are not wiser than God, nor do you have a better sense of direction than He has.

He knows what's best for your life and He knows the timing for everything. If you are not sure about a move, wait upon God until you are sure. Seek out confirmation from His Word, from prayer and from other like-minded believers. Don't forget to wait on God because He is your guide.

---

70 **You can't follow the Lord from the front.** It is ridiculous to think you can actually lead God in this life. Yet, sometimes you act like you can and are the one in charge calling the shots. You are not; the Lord is. If you jump ahead of God, life truly becomes foggy and confusing. But when you let God go before you, life becomes clear and you understand He is in control. And when you yield to Him, you will be in such a better place than if you attempted to lead your own destiny. God knows exactly where you need to go and what you need to do. You can't follow from the front. You can only follow from the back where your all-knowing Leader is before you. A good leader is someone who has learned how to be a good follower, so follow the Lord well.

71 **Sit down and seek God.** One of the best ways you can seek the Lord is to sit in a quiet place and pray. When was the last time you did that, distraction free? If it's been a while, it's time to do it again! Only then will you be able to hear His voice rather than just your own.

It's easy to talk and talk when there are voices all around because you simply have to talk a little louder. But when it comes to listening to the Lord, you need to find a quiet place to do so. This has helped me over the years like crazy. I wake up at what most people would view as an insanely early hour every day so I can get some quiet time with God. This works for me, but you know your situation and when you can steal away and seek God in a quiet place. Make this a habit and don't use the excuse that you are too busy. No child of God is ever too busy to pray to the Lord. This is how our relationship with Him fosters and grows!

_____

_____

_____

72 **Reality can only be seen if you are seeking God.** People today want to follow something or someone that is actually genuine. They don't want the drama and the fake faith that comes from those who are living shallowly. They want to live for deep, meaningful and purposeful things. When you are seeking God on a daily basis, you will truly see reality. You will understand why you were created, why you are alive, and what you are called to do on this earth and Who you are doing it for. You don't have to play any guessing games. Every single action that you take should be after you've sought God for direction and guidance. If you forsake seeking God, you forsake the spiritual side of life which is the most important part.

_____

_____

_____

73 **Tomorrow is no reason for you to worry. It's a reason for you to worship.** So often you think about what might happen tomorrow when the Lord is calling you to be thankful today. You can praise God if you wake up tomorrow because He's given you another day to live. But don't forget to praise God for your life and for leading you presently.

At this moment you are in the midst of answered prayer and therefore, are in the midst of blessings. If you don't believe me, just pause for a second and think about it. Ponder how God has used praying people in your life to point you to the Lord. Meditate on what God has truly done in your past to get you to where you are today. Seriously think about it and even write it down. The result will be gratefulness for God's great faithfulness. So those reasons to worry are not valid but those reasons to worship are real. Praise Him!

_____

_____

_____

74 **Believe and be free.** Living by faith is so easy for you to say verbally, but at times so difficult for you to live out. Those times when you feel restricted and limited are most likely the times your faith is faltering. Without faith it's impossible to please God—but without faith it's also impossible to live in freedom. As you walk by faith from day to day and on a continual basis, you'll realize that giving up control for God is a great action. The more you seek God, the less restricted your life will be because you'll be in dependence upon the Lord. There is freedom in this life and it starts with faith.

_____

_____

_____

75 **God has a beautiful purpose for you in this life.** You do not exist randomly. You are not here just to live out your life and do nothing of value or purpose. God has a purpose and divine plan for your life. He wants to use you mightily for His glory, and there is nothing more amazing than that! To walk in the middle of God's mission for you is completely beautiful because you are living out the purpose and calling that God has for you. You are not an accident. God created you, sustains you and wants to use you to spread the message that saves souls. It's beautiful to know that God created you and wants to use you radically in this life to be a truth teller. Your life matters.

_____

_____

_____

76 **You are loved.** Sometimes you forget the amazing fact that *God is love* and His deep love is directed toward you perpetually. Sometimes you don't "feel" loved by God and you question His love for you because you feel like a failure. Please abandon those thoughts and lies. God thought about you before He knit you in the womb; your life matters to Him because He created and crafted you. Don't let an unbelieving world cause you to think God doesn't care about you. Don't let your flesh doubt that your Redeemer absolutely adores you. Don't let the enemy make you question the way God feels about you. He loves you as if you were the only one He loves. You are alive, provided for and sustained because of His great love!

_____

_____

_____

77 **Comfort comes from your Creator.** There have been times when you have needed comfort and you did not get it. You attempted to find comfort and rest in a person and realized that is not possible. Sure, temporary solace is there and God uses people to console you and me. But the fact is the true source of comfort from Whom we are to take in and give out is the Creator of the universe! I can't tell you how many avenues I've taken in life to attempt to find comfort, peace and rest. After many years I realized that the only real effective comfort comes from my God! He is all you need to find rest, peace, and true solace in your heart. Seek comfort from God and relay His comfort to whoever you can!

_____

_____

_____

78 **Rest in reality.** Once in a while you attempt to find rest in this world because you forget that God is the only One in whom you can find rest! You tried and it didn't work. The reality is that it is an amazing character trait to run to the Lord and depend upon Him for life. People who don't understand may think you are weak and you should just do it all yourself with the help of some god in the air. This is an outlook stemming from those who have never had true rest from heaven. Don't let anything stop you from seeking God for heart rest and comfort. God is not just a few people's reality.

He is reality for all of humanity. Keep seeking Him and you'll be settled in your mind, in your heart and in your soul.

_____

_____

_____

79 **It's about depth over width.** The more you focus on the things of God, the deeper you will go in your relationship with Him. You are not called to strive through a spiritual checklist in order to make God happy. You are called to grow deeper in your relationship with your heavenly Father so that everything you do flows from connecting with Him on a consistent basis. You've never been in a place with such depth as your relationship with God will take you. As you seek God and throw your whole life toward living for Him, you are blessed to live for what actually matters in this short life. Give all to God and watch as you grow deeper in the faith than you have ever been before! In your walk with God it's all about depth. "May your roots go down deep into the soil of God's marvelous love" (Ephesians 3:17 TLB), being watered by God's Word.

_____

_____

_____

80 **The way to spiritually flourish is to forge ahead in the faith.** Do you want to grow in the faith and be passionately on fire for God? Consistently seeking the Lord is the way to go and to have a revived heart that longs for more of Him. God gives you all the tools you need to thrive in the faith and to progress in your one-on-one relationship with Him. You can forge ahead by staying focused on the object of your faith—the Lord Jesus Christ. Keep going forward and don't give up. Keep your eyes on Him on a daily basis and you won't sink. You'll stay afloat. Now is the time for you to walk by faith and enter into all that God has for you. Take those consistent faith steps and watch your faith flourish!

_____

_____

_____

81 **God is greater than you can see and sense.** Sometimes you don't see God as big and mighty as He actually is. When you view God as being limited, then He will do limited work in your life. But when you see Him as all-powerful, you'll know that He is able to shatter the impossible and do the miraculous. He is on the throne and you are at His feet! God is sovereign and in complete control of any situation. Therefore, you can rest easy knowing that the Lord has everything planned out and He is continually paving the way for you to fulfill your calling. Trust Him. God's sovereignty surpasses your feelings and senses. His power trumps every other outlet of strength and every other concept of might.

_____

_____

_____

82 **Believe in Him and be free from habitual sin.**
The more you pursue God and grow in your faith, the more you will view sin as disgusting and disgraceful. The enemy would attempt to have you believe that sin is good and you need to satisfy your flesh by giving in to the temptation that is hurled your way. Don't do it! Continue to be led by the Spirit so that you will walk by faith and detest sin. Habitual or continual sin has taken out so many believers who were once walking strong with God. Now they are backslidden, adrift and confused. They used to walk with the Lord, but now they are wanderers. Feed your soul with truth from God's Word and watch as He breaks the chains of unhealthy bondage in your life! It's not about maintaining your walk. It's about moving forward. Keep taking those faith steps and you'll always desire to be aligned with Him.

_____

_____

_____

83 **Seek God first and watch Him fiercely work.** As you pursue your relationship with the Creator of the universe, you will see Him do miraculous things and accomplish amazing feats! If you are living for Jesus, most likely you have already seen supernatural and incredible things! And as you remain active for God, know that it opens the door to see the Lord defeat the impossible and bust open those worldly blockades.

Seek God first and everything else in your life will line up. And more importantly, you'll see clearly what He wants you to do, where He wants you to go, and who He wants you to talk to. Putting God first means seeing Him on the throne and being at His feet in complete awe and reverence. There is no replacement or stand-in when it comes to your King being on the throne of your heart.

_____

_____

_____

84 **Depend upon the Lord and you'll deepen your walk with Him.** God will be pleased as you daily lay down your life for the One who created you. Do you want to grow deeper in your faith? Depending on the Lord is a sure way to do that. As you traverse through this life, know that walking independently from God always results in confusion, misdirection and anxiety. You've lived in that mess long enough and now it's time to break free and break through! I know you want to go deeper in your relationship with the Lord and the key to doing that is to lean into Him, bend your heart toward Him, and seek Him for every divine direction and decision. When you daily trust God, it will lead to a faith that is susceptible to serious growth!

---

85 **Clarity comes when we lean on our Creator.** The way from blurry vision to transparent clarity is through leaning all your weight on the Lord. You could be having the most confusing season of your life and things just don't seem to make sense. Maybe you are wondering why all these things are happening. But these are the moments when you should trust God, live out your faith like never before, and seek Him through prayer and His Word.

As you do, confusion will give way to understanding and questioning God will turn into trusting Him. Your life path will be illuminated when you continually pursue your Creator.

---

86 **Let the Scriptures seep into the core of who you are.** When the Bible becomes more than just words on paper, but a living love letter to your heart, the truth will seep into your being and completely transform your life. The Bible isn't just a nice book with cute little stories that make you feel good. The Scriptures are the very words of God written through His people long ago to bring encouragement to your life right now! How amazing is that?! As you delve into the biblical decrees, let the words penetrate and infiltrate your heart and transform your mind. God's Word is living and life-altering. As you read God's statutes, let them confront you, correct you, and comfort you. God is so faithful to speak through His powerful Word!

_____

_____

_____

87 **Shatter the status quo by setting your mind on things above.** The world will always go opposite of the way of God. The world will never promote Jesus, be into the gospel or share truth. You are unique in that God created you to be a conduit of Christ and a light for the Lord. God wants to use you daily for His glory and has so much more for you to do! This truth is a complete blessing! When you set your mind on things above, you will be so useful for the kingdom of God! Focus on heavenly things and make a serious impact for eternity. All glory to God!

88 **Have faith and forget the past.** As you place present faith in the Lord Jesus, your sordid past grows dim and God's glorious future for you becomes clear. You may not be able to forget everything in the past but give what has happened to the Lord and He can bring freedom to your heart. You have had hard times, but there is healing. You have had difficult seasons, but God can set you free. You have gone through insufferable storms, but God can settle your heart and give you peace no matter what. If those memories keep trying to infiltrate your soul, pray, give it to God, and repeat. The past can be used by the enemy to dishearten you, but God can use it to remind you of His faithfulness right now. Breathe easy and give it all to the Lord!

89 **Time is too short, so live for the Lord today.** This is easy to say but it can be a difficult action to take. As the years go by, you realize that time does not slow down. It actually seems to speed up and quite a bit!

The good news is that if you are reading this, you are still alive so the Lord wants to use you for His glory! Now is the time to be used for eternity. Not yesterday, not next year, but right now. Where the Lord has you at this very moment is where God wants to powerfully use you to shine His light to this lost and confused world. You are not beyond the Lord working in and through you. He still wants to do a work in your heart and as long as you are breathing, God can do the miraculous!

_____

_____

_____

90 **Creation cries out stirring you to crave a relationship with God.** As you are relaxing at the beach or enjoying the beautiful mountains, you see God's amazing handiwork all around you. Isn't it a blessing to just enjoy the Lord's creation and be reminded of how powerful, creative and amazing He is? You are joyfully overwhelmed in your heart as you stare at the stars, glimpse the sunrise or see the multitude of colors in the gorgeous sky. It is a blessing to let your surroundings bring a reassurance to your heart and mind that the Lord God is right there with you! He has created all that you see for you to enjoy and to remind you that He is a constant comfort. As you soak in the scenery that was creatively made by God, remember to thank Him, praise Him, and be awed by Him. You can see God as you gaze at His wondrous creation!

91 **Dedication to the Lord will give you clear direction from the Lord.** The Christian life is all about consistency. As you daily dedicate your life to Him, your path in life will clearly illuminate. It is such a comfort to know that God knows where you need to go and what you need to do. As you remain loyal and obedient to your heavenly Father, confusion flees and clarity results. Stay seeking God and know that as you communicate with Him, your heart and mind will be pure. The Lord has a different timetable than you, but that's OK as long as you continue seeking Him. He will give you the next step and the step after that then the step after that. Your relationship with God is all about dedication and continual commitment.

92 **God's purpose becomes clear as you peer into His precepts.** You've been frustrated about God's calling on your life. You've wondered if you are where He wants you to be and if you are doing what He wants you to do. Life seems unclear and you're super stressed. Sound familiar? We've all been in that place before and I believe the remedy is to get back into God's Word on a consistent basis.

When you neglect God's Word, you are shutting your ears off to your heavenly Father. He wants to lead you and desires that you be in the middle of His divine mission for you. Keep seeking the Lord through prayer and His Word and you will know exactly what God wants you to do and where He wants you to go. The Bible will make it completely clear. You may not see the whole story, but you will see what is in front of you and still live chapter by chapter.

_____

_____

_____

93 **Live out your faith now and uninhibitedly, because life flies by so fast.** You may think and believe that God wants to use you mightily in the future. While that may be true, the future is not yet here. God wants to use you now!

If you are waiting for some future moment when the Lord is going to finally activate your faith, you may be missing out on what God wants to do in and through you today. So live like today is the last day He is giving you and you will grow to produce spiritual fruit.

With that on the forefront of your mind, go all in for Him and watch Him work! Waiting for some future moment when you are comfortable and everything lines up is over. Let God use you where you are presently, now and today.

_____

_____

_____

94 **Put to death the past and plow ahead into the future**. The way to grow in the faith is to let past weights go. There may have been times you let the past pull you into a dark and regretful place. You feel guilt, shame and regret. You cringe at the thought of what you did and it stunts your growth today.

Let those past weights go and don't be brought into a dark place anymore. God has delivered you and is with you, working in your heart and reshaping your life. Be confident in Christ. He hasn't wasted your past. He wants to use it as a beautiful testimony to help others navigate through the same things!

So don't stay stuck in your past but use it for God's glory. Put to death the feelings of shame, condemnation and guilt, and live instead in forgiveness. Now grab forgiveness as a mantle of truth and forge ahead in the faith!

_____

_____

_____

95 **God's plan becomes plain as we press into His promises.** Every single promise that God has given you has come to pass or will come to pass. There may be things you have been praying about that have not yet come to fruition, but the Lord knows all about them.

You need to keep waiting and praying. Pressing into His promises means you lean upon the Lord for the outcome of what you've been praying for. So are you fully trusting in Him? Are you believing He will come through? Are you having faith that God will fulfill His promises?

To walk by faith means you answer yes to all these questions. God's plans are perfect and as you follow Him, He will impart to you the steps you should take and the direction you should go. Keep on the path He is paving for you and don't give up. God always comes through!

_____

_____

_____

96 **God will always be and has always been.** From before the beginning of time, the Lord has always existed. He created you because He absolutely loves you!

Maybe you have had moments and seasons that have been unsettling and inconsistent. You have had storms that have clouded your vision and everything was up in the air. In these moments you need to remember who God is! Remember He is your foundation.

You can depend upon Him every second of every day. You can trust Him and know that no matter how unconformable and unconventional life gets, He is your constant. He is there for you and loves you always—today just as much as He loved you yesterday.

_____

_____

_____

97 **The simple gospel changes your life and ministers to you.** Jesus died and rose again so you could be saved and set apart to live for Him. It's such a powerful truth that you need to revisit it again and again to remind yourself why you are so blessed.

This gospel message is simple yet profound, and any time you complicate it the results are disastrous. God has not called you to complicate the truth, but to share it simply and in love.

Yes, there are times when it's difficult and awkward to share, but even then you are to relay the truth from God! How amazing and beautiful is it that we can?! Share the gospel and keep it simple.

98 **Truth may not be popular, but it leads to your God-given purpose.** You know the way to be saved and you know the Lord who saves. There are so many people who resist the truth; they follow lies instead. As you've been transformed by the truth from God, you are now given a path to follow. You have a purpose from God and it is glorious! It may not seem like it's glorious, but once you settle in and learn to be content right where God has you, then He can use you for His glory!

God reveals to you every day what He wants you to do and what your daily purpose actually is. You matter and the Lord loves you so much that He desires to use you to be a light and an active kingdom participant. What a blessing!

99 **Memories are moments we can reflect upon and praise God for.** When you remember God's radical work in your life, it blesses you like crazy. Each step you see how you were being called to a higher purpose and how things you had been through could now be used as a testimony to His faithfulness!

God clearly has brought you through the roughest of times imaginable, and for that you can be eternally grateful. You can even reflect on how He has worked in your life in this past year. Even if it's been more difficult than ever, just know the Lord is working in your heart and in your life.

_____

_____

_____

100 **As life flies by, remember to praise the Father.** Every year seems to race by more quickly than the last. It seems like time is speeding up and you wonder, *What has happened to the last ten years? They were here and now they are gone!*

In light of this, know that your time on earth will not last forever. You are here and then you are gone. There's no need to see this truth in a pessimistic light, but rather it should spur you on to live for the Lord that much more!

Praise God for every day you wake up and every week you make it through with His wisdom and strength. Time does fly by but every day is a great blessing from your heavenly Father. So don't forget to praise Him for His faithfulness and truth "for He is good! For His mercy endures forever" (Psalm 136:1).

_____

_____

_____

CONCLUSION

I pray that as you continue in your walk with the Lord that He would continue to speak to your heart and refine your life. We can be confident that the Lord will complete the work that He has begun in each of our hearts (Philippians 1:6). I encourage you to seek the Lord in prayer, continue in His Word and fellowship with a body of like-minded believers. God is not done with you!

www.ingramcontent.com/pod-product-compliance
Lightning Source LLC
Chambersburg PA
CBHW071931020426
42331CB00010B/2824